What Lives in the Dirt?

CENTIPEDES AND MILLIPEDES

CRABTREE
PUBLISHING COMPANY
WWW.CRABTREEBOOKS.COM

CRABTREE
PUBLISHING COMPANY
WWW.CRABTREEBOOKS.COM

Published in Canada
Crabtree Publishing
616 Welland Avenue
St. Catharines, ON
L2M 5V6

Published in the United States
Crabtree Publishing
PMB 59051
350 Fifth Ave, 59th Floor
New York, NY 10118

Published in 2020 by Crabtree Publishing Company

First published in Great Britain in 2019 by Wayland
Copyright © Hodder and Stoughton, 2019

Printed in the U.S.A./122019/CG20191101

Author: Susie Williams

Editorial director: Kathy Middleton

Editors: Victoria Brooker, Ellen Rodger

Designer: Lisa Peacock

Illustrator: Hannah Tolson

Production coordinator and prepress: Margaret Salter

Print coordinator: Katherine Berti

Library and Archives Canada Cataloguing in Publication

Title: Centipedes and millipedes / by Susie Williams
  and [illustrated by] Hannah Tolson.
Names: Williams, Susie, author. | Tolson, Hannah, illustrator.
Description: Series statement: What lives in the dirt? |
  Previously published: London: Wayland, 2019. | Includes index.
Identifiers: Canadiana (print) 20190195088 |
  Canadiana (ebook) 20190195096
  ISBN 9780778773870 (hardcover) |
  ISBN 9780778773962 (softcover) |
  ISBN 9781427125026 (HTML)
Subjects: LCSH: Centipedes—Juvenile literature. |
  LCSH: Millipedes—Juvenile literature.
Classification: LCC QL449 .W55 2020 | DDC j595.6—dc23

Library of Congress Cataloging-in-Publication Data

Names: Williams, Susie, author. | Tolson, Hannah, illustrator.
Title: Centipedes and millipedes / by Susie Williams and
  Hannah Tolson.
Description: New York : Crabtree Publishing Company, 2020. |
  Series: What lives in the dirt? | Includes index.
Identifiers: LCCN 2019043938 (print) | LCCN 2019043939 (ebook)
  ISBN 9780778773870 (hardcover) |
  ISBN 9780778773962 (paperback) |
  ISBN 9781427125026 (ebook)
Subjects: LCSH: Centipedes--Juvenile literature. |
  Millipedes--Juvenile literature.
Classification: LCC QL449.5 .W54 2020 (print) |
  LCC QL449.5 (ebook) | DDC   595.6/2--dc23
LC record available at https://lccn.loc.gov/2019043938
LC ebook record available at https://lccn.loc.gov/2019043939

What Lives in the Dirt?

CENTIPEDES AND MILLIPEDES

By Susie Williams and Hannah Tolson

Centipedes and millipedes live
in damp, dark places.

Look for them underneath stones,
fallen leaves, and rotting logs.

Centipedes have flat bodies.

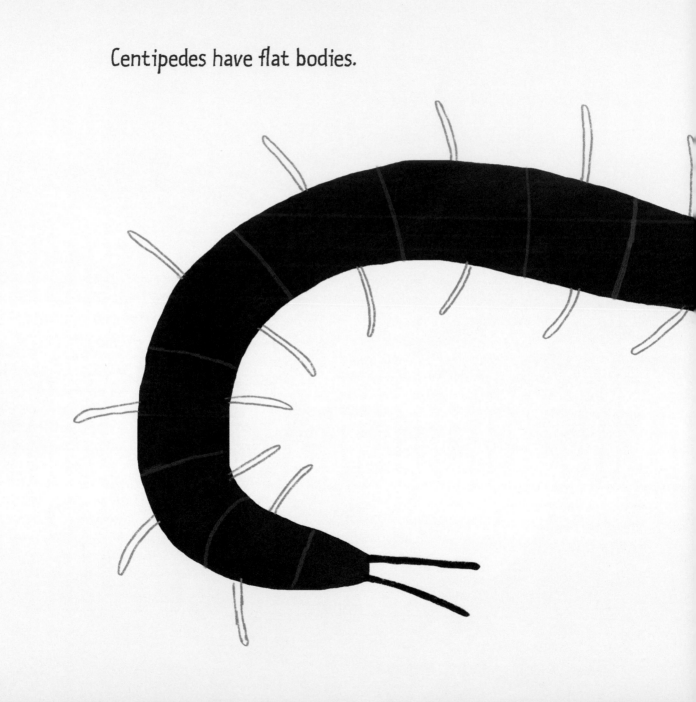

They have long **antennas** on the front
and long legs at the back.

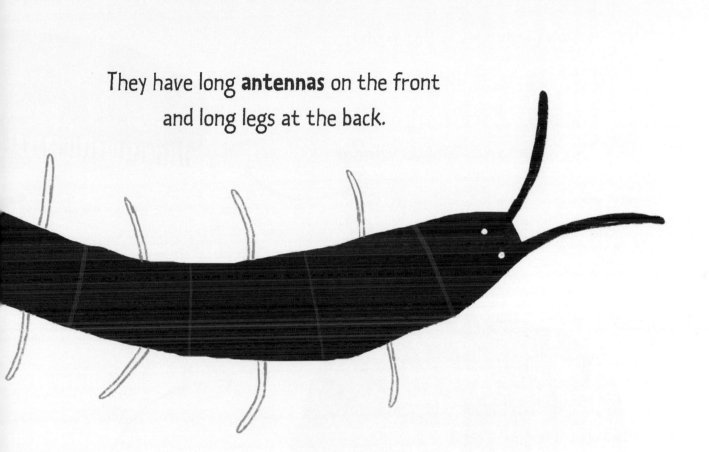

It is hard to tell which end is which!

There are many different types of millipedes. Some millipedes have bodies shaped like a **cylinder**.

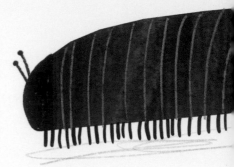

Pill millipedes have rounded bodies. They look a lot like pillbugs.

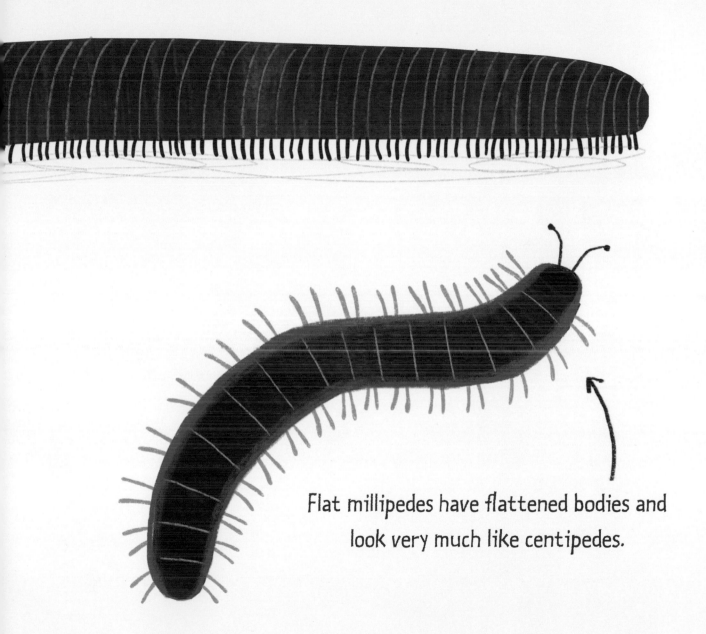

Flat millipedes have flattened bodies and look very much like centipedes.

Centipede and millipede bodies are
made up of parts called **segments**.
Centipedes have one pair of legs
on each segment.

Centipedes can have over 100 legs,
but most have just 30.

Millipedes have two pairs
of legs on each segment.

Millipedes have between
80 and 400 legs!

Centipedes and millipedes are nocturnal.
That means they are mainly active at night.

They don't like heat. That is why you are
more likely to see them at night when it is cool,
or after it has rained.

If it is too hot, they will dig down
into the soil to keep cool.

Birds and toads love to
eat centipedes
and millipedes.

When a centipede feels threatened,
it quickly skitters away to hide beneath
a nearby log or stone.

Millipedes curl
themselves up tightly
to protect themselves.

15

Centipedes have **poisonous** claws on each side of their head. They use these to catch food, such as insects, spiders, and slugs.

The claws also help them defend themselves from attack. If you picked up a centipede, they might pinch you with their claws. But don't worry—their poison is harmless to humans.

Millipedes usually eat dead plants and leaves.

But sometimes you can find them chowing
down on juicy fruits or vegetables,
such as strawberries and tomatoes.

Centipedes and millipedes are found
all over the world. Some centipedes
glow in the dark!

Geophilus electricus

The Indian tiger centipede is black and orange.

The largest centipede in the world is found in South America. It grows up to 12 inches (30 cm) long.

Around the world, there are many different types of millipedes.

Red millipede

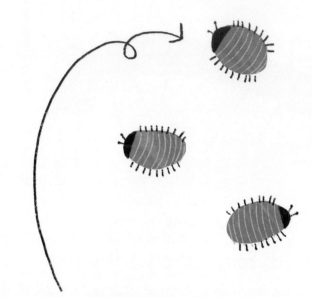

Madagascan green-emerald pill millipedes

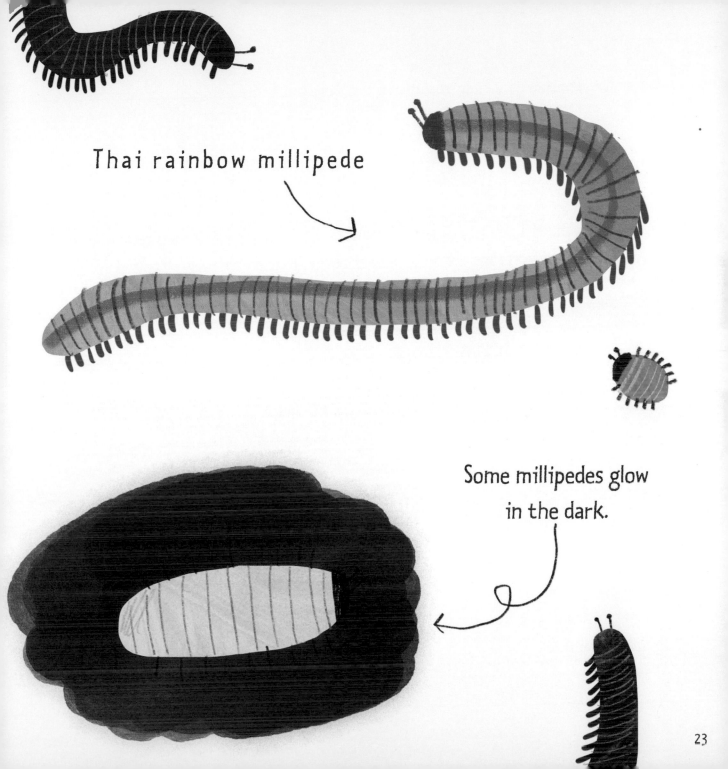

Thai rainbow millipede

Some millipedes glow
in the dark.

Centipedes and millipedes
have poor eyesight.

They use their antennas to help them
feel their way around.

Watch closely and you'll see their
antennas tap the ground
as they move along.

Gardeners like centipedes and millipedes. Centipedes eat **garden pests** such as slugs and small insects.

Millipedes eat dead leaves and plants,
removing them from the ground. See if
you can spot any centipedes or millipedes.

Watch millipedes close up

Make a home for a millipede and look after one for a week.

1. Put leaves and soil on the bottom of your container. Your container will need a cover to stop the millipede from crawling out. The lid must contain air holes.

2. Put the container in a cool, shady place.

3. At **dusk**, go outside and look for a millipede. Lift up logs and stones to find one. If you gently touch a millipede, it will curl up and this will make it easier to pick up. Carefully place one in the container.

4. Feed your millipede with small pieces of chopped up fruit or vegetables.

5. Spray some water into the container every day.

You will need:
- a glass container, such as an old aquarium or terrarium
- a container cover with small holes in the top for air
- small pieces of fruit or vegetables

Now you can watch your millipede close up and see how it moves and eats. You should notice that it stays curled up during the day and becomes more active at night.

After a few days, carefully put the millipede back in the wild where you found it.

More amazing facts about centipedes and millipedes

The words centipede and millipede are based on Latin words. *Centi* means 100, *milli* means 1,000 and *pede* means feet.

Centipedes will always have an odd number of pairs of legs, which means it's actually not possible for a centipede to have 100 legs.

Centipedes can grow new legs to replace those that are lost. If a bird bites off a centipede's leg, the centipede might be able to escape and regrow the lost leg.

If you still can't tell them apart, then touch them. Centipedes will run away and millipedes will curl up.

Glossary

antennas – Pair of long, thin body parts on the head of insects and other animals that allow them to sense or feel

cylinder – A shape that has one curved side with a circle on each end, such as a can

dusk – Early part of the evening

garden pests – Insects and bugs that eat plants, often causing the plants to die

poisonous – Having a substance that can cause death or illness to others

segment – One of the parts into which something is, or can be, separated

Index